George Washington

By Barbara L. Luciano

PEARSON
Scott Foresman

Editorial Offices: Glenview, Illinois • Parsippany, New Jersey • New York, New York
Sales Offices: Needham, Massachusetts • Duluth, Georgia • Glenview, Illinois
Coppell, Texas • Sacramento, California • Mesa, Arizona

This is George Washington.

He lived long ago.

He was our President.

He had a big job.

February
Sunday Monday Tuesday Wednesday Thursday Friday Saturday
1 2 3 4 5 6
7 8 9 10 11 12 13
14 15 16 17 18 19 20
21 22 23 24 25 26 27
28

This is his birthday.

The President still has a big job.

Glossary

President the leader of our country